The Brothers Grimm

by Joann Mulvaney Messier

HOUGHTON MIFFLIN HARCOURT
School Publishers

ILLUSTRATION CREDIT: **4** Joe LeMonnier / Melissa Turk

PHOTOGRAPHY CREDITS: **Cover** (frame) © Image Farm / Antique Frames, (inset) © Bettmann/CORBIS; **1** © Archivo Iconografico, S.A. / Corbis; **3** © Gianni Dagli Orti / Corbis; **4** © Mary Evans Picture Library / Alamy; **8–9** © INTERFOTO Pressebildagentur / Alamy; **9** © Bettmann/Corbis; **11** © PhotoDisc / Metaphors; **12** © PhotoDisc / Just Documents; **13** © North Wind Picture Archives / Alamy; **14** © PhotoDisc / Script and Texture; **15** © Archivo Iconografico, S.A. / Corbis; **16** (top) © INTERFOTO Pressebildagentur / Alamy, (bottom) © INTERFOTO Pressebildagentur / Alamy; **17** © Bettmann / Corbis. **Tab** © Shutterstock

Printed in China

ISBN-13: 978-0-547-02472-1
ISBN-10: 0-547-02472-X

4 5 6 7 8 0940 18 17 16 15 14 13 12
4500351679

Table of Contents

Introduction

"Once upon a time . . ." When someone speaks this age-old phrase, you know that you are going to hear a fairy tale. Today we think of fairy tales as bedtime stories for children. The hero or heroine faces danger but "lives happily ever after" in the end. Evildoers are punished. You may be surprised to learn that fairy tales have a long and sometimes dark history.

A poet in the Middle Ages tells a heroic legend to a group of eager listeners.

Many centuries ago, common people told stories from memory. Women often told these folktales while they worked at spinning, weaving, and sewing. Families passed the tales from one generation to the next.

In the 16th and 17th centuries, Italian and French writers began to collect folk stories and write them down. Many of the tales were violent and gruesome. To appeal to upper-class readers, writers took out unpleasant details and added moral lessons.

In the 1800s, two German brothers developed a different approach. Jacob and Wilhelm Grimm wanted to preserve folktales just as the common folk told them. Their work would have far-reaching and lasting effects.

Where Are the Fairies?

The term *fairy tale* was invented in 1697 by a French woman named Madame d'Aulnoy. She wrote a popular collection of stories called *Tales of the Fairies*. Later writers picked up this term. They used it to describe certain kinds of folktales. Fairy tales share features such as an unreal setting, unusual characters, and magical events. One feature that all fairy tales do *not* share is the presence of fairies!

Fairy tales often include magical creatures.

Growing Up Grimm

The story of the Brothers Grimm begins in the small town of Hanau, in what is now Germany. Jacob was born in 1785, and his brother Wilhelm was born a year later. Jacob and Wilhelm were the oldest of six children. Their father, Philipp Grimm, was a lawyer in Hanau. The children's mother, Dorothea, took care of the house and children with the help of servants.

In 1791, the family moved to the small city of Steinau. There, Philipp Grimm took the position of district judge. Jacob and Wilhelm studied with tutors. They learned reading, writing, math, and French.

In their free time, the boys went on long walks through the historic town. They explored the surrounding countryside and ancient forests, wandering through old castles, towers, and medieval monuments.

Jacob and Wilhelm always had a close bond. They enjoyed snowball fights, hide-and-seek, and other childhood games. Both boys enjoyed collecting and sketching insects and plants. They also formed the habit of copying passages from books. Little did the brothers know that these boyhood interests would be so useful to the work they would do as adults!

In January 1796, Philipp Grimm died suddenly of pneumonia. Jacob was 11 years old, and Wilhelm was 10. Life changed dramatically for the family. Their mother had to care for six young children on her own.

The Grimm family had lived comfortably, but now they faced money troubles. They moved to a smaller home and had to give up their servants. As the oldest child, Jacob did everything he could to help out.

School and University

Dorothea was determined to give her children a good education. Her sister helped, providing money to send Jacob and Wilhelm to school. In 1798, the boys left their family to attend the Lyceum, in Kassel. It was an excellent school.

Jacob and Wilhelm studied hard to succeed in school. During this time, the brothers grew even closer. Their hard work paid off. Both boys became top scholars.

This map shows several cities that were important in the Grimm brothers' lives. As you continue reading, note what happened in Kassel and Marburg.

Places to See in Germany

If you ever get a chance to tour Germany, here are two towns to visit with connections to the Brothers Grimm:

- **Hanau** — The Grimm home in Hanau was destroyed during World War II. Today, a bronze statue of Jacob and Wilhelm Grimm stands in front of Hanau's city hall to honor their life and work.
- **Steinau** — The Grimm family home in Steinau is now a museum dedicated to the Brothers Grimm.

In 1802, Jacob left to study at the University of Marburg. He chose to study law, like his father. The brothers found the separation difficult. Jacob was often bored by his law classes. He missed his brother.

Wilhelm stayed at Kassel to finish his studies. However, he had a serious asthma attack and could not study for months. During this time, he was allowed only to sketch and draw. Still, Wilhelm finished his studies ahead of time. In 1803, after a year apart, Wilhelm joined Jacob at the University of Marburg. He also chose to study law.

The brothers were not alike in every way. Jacob had sharp features and was short and strong. He had a tendency to be quiet, thoughtful, and very studious. Wilhelm had softer features and was taller than Jacob. Wilhelm was also more outgoing, although he, too, was studious.

New Directions

Jacob and Wilhelm became friends with Friedrich Karl von Savigny, a law professor. Savigny sparked their interest in history, literature, and the German language. Another friend, Clemens Brentano, inspired the brothers with a love of folk poetry. These interests began to lead the Grimms away from careers in law. They would take another path.

In 1805, Savigny went to Paris to research a book about Roman law. Soon he asked Jacob to come to Paris to help with the work. Once again, the Grimm brothers faced a separation. Jacob enjoyed his time in Paris, but he missed his brother.

Wilhelm, too, felt lonely without Jacob. The brothers kept in touch through letters. In October 1805, Jacob returned to Marburg. Jacob and Wilhelm were overjoyed to be together again. Then they traveled to Kassel. Their mother, brothers, sister, and aunt now lived there. For the first time in years, the Grimm family was reunited.

The city of Marburg is built on a hill. The Grimm brothers would have been very familiar with the city's steep streets, stairways, and alleys.

While Wilhelm continued his studies at Marburg, Jacob looked for work. He felt responsible for the welfare of his family. In 1806, Jacob found a job with the government's war office. The pay was not good, and the work was dull. But there was an even bigger problem. Jacob had to wear an uncomfortable uniform and a powdered wig!

Wilhelm (left) and Jacob Grimm

Difficult Times

Later that fall, life in Kassel changed dramatically. The French, under Napoleon, took over much of Prussia, as Germany was then called. Political tension was high. Napoleon made Kassel the capital of a new kingdom, Westphalia. He made his youngest brother, Jérôme, king.

The next few years were difficult for the Grimm family. Jacob and Wilhelm struggled to find work. In May 1808, Dorothea Grimm died. The family now had to go on without their beloved mother. The small pension they received from their father's work also ended.

Jacob finally found work as director of King Jérôme's private library. The position paid well. It also gave Jacob free time to study what interested him. The Grimm family finally had some financial security. Wilhelm, however, still had not found work. His health was poor.

As Jacob worked to support the family and Wilhelm worked to regain his health, the brothers kept up their interest in old German literature and folktales. They had written about folktales in journals. Now they began to seek out tales and write them down. The Grimms genuinely hoped that the old tales would restore pride to the German people, whose mood was predominantly gloomy under French occupation.

Dorothea Viehmann

An innkeeper's daughter was one of the Grimms' most important sources for old tales. Dorothea Viehmann gave the brothers more than 40 tales. Dorothea was a widow when she met the Grimms. She told them stories she had heard travelers tell at her father's inn.

According to Wilhelm, Dorothea had a true gift for recalling tales. She repeated each story exactly the same way each time. One of her stories was "Aschenputtel." This is the story we know as "Cinderella."

Collecting the Tales

From the aspect, or viewpoint, of the brothers, the most difficult part of their work was finding the old tales. The stories had been told time and time again, but most people had never thought to write them down. Jacob and Wilhelm sometimes turned to written works. More often, though, they tried to find storytellers who could repeat the stories.

The tales came from a variety of sources. Soldiers, shepherds, and other country people recounted tales from memory. Other tales came from old school friends and neighbors in Kassel. Sometimes Jacob and Wilhelm made trips to meet with a storyteller who seemed especially promising.

In collecting the tales, Jacob and Wilhelm's old study habits and attention to detail proved very useful. They tried to write down everything just as the storyteller said it. They included in their collection only tales that they believed were truly German.

A Favor for a Friend

In 1806, Clemens Brentano was working on a collection of German literature. He asked Jacob and Wilhelm for some folktales. In a few years, the brothers collected 49 tales. But Brentano never published his collection. So, in 1812, the Grimm brothers decided to publish a collection of their own stories. A favor for a friend had started them along the path they would follow for the rest of their lives.

Publishing the Tales

In 1812, Jacob and Wilhelm published Volume One of their work. In English, the book was called *Children's and Household Tales*. The stories were for both children and adults. There were 86 tales in the first volume, including "The Frog King," "Rapunzel," "Cinderella," "Snow White," and "Hansel and Gretel." The book also included a long introduction and many footnotes. It did not have any illustrations.

A German edition of *Children's and Household Tales*

Sales of the book were slow. People said the stories were too violent. Some thought the themes were too mature for children. Others suggested that the book should be illustrated.

As Jacob and Wilhelm continued to collect tales, Napoleon began to lose power throughout Europe. In 1813, the French withdrew from Kassel. Jacob turned his attention to diplomatic work. Meanwhile, Wilhelm continued working on the second volume of *Children's and Household Tales*. It was published in 1815. This volume included 70 tales.

Key Events in the Brothers' Lives

1785
Jacob Grimm is born January 4, in Hanau.

1786
Wilhelm Grimm is born February 24, in Hanau.

1791
The Grimm family moves to Steinau.

1796
Philipp Grimm, their father, dies January 10.

1806
Jacob and Wilhelm begin to collect folktales.

1808
Dorothea Grimm, their mother, dies May 27.

1812
The brothers publish Volume One of *Children's and Household Tales*.

1814-15
Volume Two of *Children's and Household Tales* is published.

1825
Wilhelm marries Henrietta Wild.

1859
Wilhelm dies, December 16.

1863
Jacob dies, September 20.

1960s
Grimms' *German Dictionary* completed.

Working and Living Together

Wilhelm took on responsibility for later editions of *Children's and Household Tales*. In response to criticism, he re-worked some of the stories. He also removed stories that seemed very violent. He wanted the tales to appeal to both children and parents. An excellent editor, Wilhelm wove lessons about life into the stories. He made the stories come alive with vivid, descriptive language.

In 1825, the brothers published another collection of tales. It was aptly named the *Small Edition*. This book included only 50 stories. But it also included illustrations by Wilhelm and Jacob's brother Ludwig. Children loved this version of the Grimms' tales. The book was very successful and was reprinted several times.

This illustration shows a scene from the Grimms' fairy tale "The Star Coins." A girl who is very poor gives away all her possessions to help others. She is rewarded when stars fall from heaven and turn to coins, making her rich.

During the brothers' lifetime, they published five more editions of *Children's and Household Tales*. The 1857 edition included 200 tales and 10 "Children's Legends."

Jacob Grimm

Wilhelm Grimm

In many ways, Jacob and Wilhelm led almost parallel lives. They shared the same interests and they usually lived, studied, and worked side by side. Together, the brothers published many books and articles. In later years, both worked as librarians and professors.

In 1825, Wilhelm married Dorothea Wild and started a family. Still, the brothers remained very close. Jacob, who never married, lived with Wilhelm and his family. As they had done when they were young, Jacob and Wilhelm worked side by side in a shared study. In their lifetimes, the two brothers published more than 35 books.

In their later years, Jacob and Wilhelm began to write the *German Dictionary*. It was a huge project, and they were not able to finish it. Wilhelm died in 1859. He was 73 years old. Jacob died four years later. When Jacob died, he was still working on the dictionary. It was finally completed by other editors in the 1960s.

Making Connections

The work of the Brothers Grimm inspired people around the world to preserve their ancient tales. People began to appreciate the connections between history and cultural traditions. For example:

- Traditional tales from the Caribbean and Latin America tell stories about the gods of the Mayas and Aztecs. They also reveal the influence of explorers, invaders, and settlers from foreign lands.
- Africans taken into slavery and brought to the Americas carried tales with them. We know this because the trickster spider, Anansi, a popular character in West African folktales, is also found in tales of the Caribbean.

A Lasting Legacy

Although the Grimm brothers were not the first to record traditional tales, they deserve credit for creating the first major collection of German tales. Their work introduced people around the world to German stories that had been passed down for years and years. Their collections also sparked an interest in folktales and fairy tales from other parts of the world. The Grimms' method for gathering tales was an innovation that others would try to imitate.

The fairy tales that Jacob and Wilhelm Grimm collected have been translated into more than 160 languages. Characters and ideas from their tales can be found today in books, plays, cartoons, feature films, and advertisements. Their work continues to influence and inspire writers, artists, moviemakers, and, most of all, children of all ages.

In 1937, Walt Disney released the animated film *Snow White and the Seven Dwarfs*. This fairy tale about a beautiful young girl and her jealous stepmother was adapted from the Grimms' tale. The film version included songs and added details to the original tale. The dwarfs, for example, now had descriptive names, such as Sneezy, Happy, and Dopey. The Grimms might not have approved of these changes in the old tale. But they, too, had changed the tales they collected.

The Grimms started their work to preserve traditional German folktales. They might have been surprised to know that their tales would spread far beyond Germany and influence people around the world!

Responding

TARGET SKILL **Fact and Opinion** What are some facts and opinions related to *The Brothers Grimm*? Copy the chart below. In the first column, write some facts from the text. For each fact, write a related opinion based on the text.

Facts	Opinions
Early folktales were often violent.	Early folktales didn't appeal to many readers.
Jacob and Wilhelm studied hard in school.	?
?	?

Write About It

Text to Text Fairy tales have unusual settings, characters, and events. Think of a character from a fairy tale you know. Write a fictional paragraph in which your character is involved in an unusual event.

TARGET VOCABULARY

aptly	parallel
aspect	predominantly
credit	tendency
genuinely	tension
innovation	welfare

TARGET SKILL **Fact and Opinion** Decide whether an idea can be proved or is a feeling or belief.

TARGET STRATEGY **Summarize** Briefly tell the important parts of the text in your own words.

GENRE **Biography** tells about events in a person's life, written by another person.